Love Kills Slowly
CROSS-STITCH

30 Cross-Stitch Patterns from Ed Hardy

Andrews McMeel
Publishing, LLC

Kansas City • Sydney • London

Contents

INTRODUCTION

This ain't your grandma's cross-stitch book.

No cutesy babies, gingerbread houses, and jack-o'-lanterns here. Cross-stitch gets a modern twist as 30 bold graphic designs from wildly popular tattoo artist Ed Hardy are turned into cross-stitch patterns. From skulls and snakes to daggers, roses, and much more, these designs are a modern take on cross-stitch.

It's hard to exactly replicate the depth and richness of an Ed Hardy design. To achieve that level of exactness, you'd need hundreds of colors of embroidery floss, often for just a stitch or two before switching to another color. Each pattern here has been created to preserve as much of the beautiful detail of the original artwork as possible while keeping it accessible for even beginning stitchers. Love may kill slowly, but you don't want to feel like cross-stitching is having the same effect.

If you want to personalize your pieces with your own words, the Ed Hardy alphabet has been included here so that you can add your favorite sayings, expressions, or names to each stitched piece. So go ahead and personalize that new cross-stitch piece with your boyfriend's name, and if you change boyfriends, you can always rip it out and redo it. (At least changing your cross-stitch is cheaper, easier, and less painful than trying to change that tattoo.)

With your finished designs, you can make your best friend a snake wall hanging, your mom a personalized dagger pillow, or your grandma a skull tea towel. To add a personal touch, you can use cross-stitch to embellish everything from baby clothes and bibs to tablecloths and dishtowels—plus, no sewing required! Love may kill slowly, but time will fly by as you create these 30 cool designs from one of the world's hottest artists.

Cross-Stitch How-To

Supplies

Cross-stitching only requires a few basic supplies. You will need the following items to create the cross-stitch designs in this book:

- Cross-stitch fabric in the appropriate size (leave 4 inches of extra fabric on each side—or more, depending on your project) as well as count (typically 14-count). Each pattern in this book specifies the count of the fabric.
- A tapestry needle, size 24 or 26 (A regular embroidery needle would be fine but a tapestry needle has a blunt tip, which is more convenient for cross-stitching.)
- Scissors
- Embroidery floss (the most commons brands are DMC or Anchor) in the colors called for in your pattern. Each pattern here lists suggested color numbers from DMC, the most commonly available embroidery floss. The titles of the colors are for convenience only and may vary. When in doubt, follow the numbers and use your best judgment when selecting colors for your project.
- Wooden or plastic hoop, if desired, to help hold your fabric taut while you stitch

Reading the Patterns and Symbol Keys

Each project in this book features a picture of an original Ed Hardy artwork in cross-stitch, a pattern grid with symbols to follow, and a symbol key.

The instructions for each project tell you what type of fabric you will need (14-count), the number of stitches across and up and down, the finished size of the project (in inches and centimeters), the recommended number of embroidery floss strands to use for each stitch, and a chart of symbols and their corresponding thread colors. Some patterns are more complicated than others, with more symbols to follow, and sometimes the symbols are similar—such as an open triangle and a solid triangle. Read the pattern carefully to make sure you're using the right color.

STARTING OFF

First, find the center of your pattern (marked here with a red cross + symbol) and the center of your fabric. To find the center of your fabric, fold it in half lengthwise and gently press the seam with your finger. Unfold and repeat the previous step widthwise. The point where the two folds meet is the approximate center of your fabric.

Next determine what color of embroidery floss is needed at the center of your pattern. Most embroidery floss is made up of six strands. Separate the strands and thread the required number (listed in the symbol key) of the correct color through your tapestry needle. Start cross-stitching at the center of your fabric and count from the corresponding red cross at the center of the pattern to determine the correct number of stitches.

MAKING A CROSS-STITCH

Cross-stitch fabric is specially created for cross-stitching. Look closely at how the fibers are arranged to create a square grid with tiny holes separating each square. In cross-stitching, the basic cross-stitch is created by forming an X pattern over one of the squares. To stitch a cross-stitch, bring your needle from the back of the fabric through to the front in the lower left corner of the square you're cross-stitching. Next, bring the needle across the square to the upper right corner forming a half stitch (/). Then, from the back of the fabric push your needle through the lower right corner and pull the embroidery floss through. And, finally, bring the needle across the square to the upper left corner and pull the needle through. You should have a single X now on the center of your fabric in the correct color.

If you have a horizontal sequence of stitches that are all the same color, you can stitch a half stitch (/) for each stitch in the row and then return to your starting point by placing the opposite half stitch (\) in sequence. This process can allow you to stitch horizontal rows quickly and efficiently as you get used to cross-stitching. If you prefer to not use this technique, you can always stitch each X one by one.

MAKING A THREE-QUARTER STITCH

A three-quarter stitch allows a pattern to show a smoother, rounded edge. To create a three-quarter stitch, start as before with your needle in the lower left corner of your square, but this time bring your needle through the center of the square through the fabric. This will create a quarter stitch. To complete the stitch, pull your needle and floss through the lower right corner and then across the square to the upper left corner. It is important to note that a three-quarter stitch can be created four different ways, since each corner of the square could be the "half" corner, depending on which edge of the piece you are working on. Look at your pattern carefully to see what is needed.

STARTING AND ENDING THREAD COLORS

When beginning a new color, leave a 1-inch tail, holding it against the back of the fabric and working over it to secure the thread. When you finish with that color, cut off about 5 inches of the thread and use your needle to weave it through the back of your work to secure it.

If this method proves too complicated, you can always tie a simple knot in the thread as an alternative.

ADDING A BACKSTITCH

Backstitching is used to outline, add details, or stitch letters or numbers on a cross-stitch piece. Backstitching can be done with a single strand of embroidery floss, but some patterns, like the ones here, ask for more. Check each pattern to see how many strands are needed. For a different look, you can increase or decrease the number of strands according to your preference.

To create the backstitch, start with your needle behind the fabric and pull it through the fabric where your backstitch line starts. Push the needle through the fabric one square in the direction of your line. Next, pull the needle through the back of the fabric and push it through the fabric one square ahead again. This will create one visible line on the front of your fabric and one visible line on the back. With your needle pulled through the fabric on the front one square ahead, push it through back one square so that the line meets up with the previously stitched line. Now bring the needle from the back to the front two squares ahead of your line and back across the front one square back.

This process creates a single, smoothly stitched line on the front and a rather looping doubled line on the back.

COMPLETING YOUR PROJECT

Once you are finished with your project, make sure all loose threads are secured, then hand wash it carefully in cold water and use a flat towel to press out the excess water. Then, lay it flat to dry.

When your work is dry, you can frame it or sew it into a pillow, shirt, baby bib, tea towel, or quilt—use your imagination!

EMBELLISHING YOUR PROJECT

As you gain confidence in your cross-stitching skills, you may want to take it to the next level by adding sequins, beads, and other embellishments. You may want to use your pattern to plan out where to put the embellishments, marking it accordingly. Make sure your tapestry needle will fit through the openings of the embellishments. If not, you may need to thread the embroidery floss through a beading needle each time you wish to add an embellishment. Then, simply slip the embellishment through the needle and complete your next stitch.

You can also embellish your piece once it is finished. You'll want a beading needle and thread in the same color as the embroidery thread on which you're sewing the embellishments. Take care to hide your knots so they don't show.

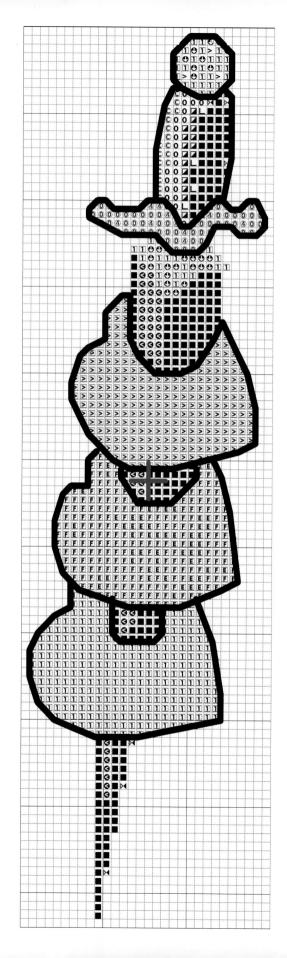

Three Hearts Dagger

Instructions and Symbol Key

Fabric: 14 count
Stitches: 28 x 102
Size: 2.00 x 7.29 inches or 5.08 x 18.51 centimeters
Colors: DMC

Use 2 strands of thread for cross-stitch.

Symbol	No.	Color Name
⓪	307	Lemon
■	310	Black
▷	341	Light blue violet
⏱	606	Bright orange-red
◩	702	Kelly green
>	720	Dark orange spice
④	726	Light topaz
E	894	Very light carnation
O	913	Medium Nile green
1	946	Medium burnt orange
F	957	Pale geranium
L	3362	Dark pine green
©	3747	Very light blue violet
◲	3799	Very dark pewter gray
◁	White	White

Use 6 strands of thread for backstitch.

	310	Black

Blue Bird

Instructions and Symbol Key

Fabric: 14 count
Stitches: 108 x 78
Size: 7.71 x 5.57 inches or 19.59 x 14.15 centimeters
Colors: DMC

Use 2 strands of thread for cross-stitch.

Symbol	No.	Color Name
■	310	Black
>	352	Light coral
P	519	Sky blue
×	535	Very light ash gray
◐	646	Dark beaver gray
↓	647	Medium beaver gray
8	648	Light beaver gray
U	712	Cream
©	727	Very light topaz
Ⓜ	745	Light pale yellow
N	747	Very light sky blue
M	762	Very light pearl gray
◢	934	Black avocado green
Ⓨ	3743	Very light antique violet
9	3761	Light sky blue
—	3845	Medium bright turquoise
D	3846	Light bright turquoise
X	3865	Winter white
∅	White	White

Use 6 strands of thread for backstitch.

	310	Black

Blue Butterfly

Instructions and Symbol Key

FABRIC: 14 count
STITCHES: 58 x 102
SIZE: 4.14 x 7.29 inches or 10.52 x 18.51 centimeters
COLORS: DMC

Use 2 strands of thread for cross-stitch.

SYMBOL	No.	COLOR NAME
⌐	165	Very light moss green
■	310	Black
7	518	Light wedgewood
▷	563	Light jade
4	564	Very light jade
S	580	Dark moss green
A	581	Moss green
✕	597	Turquoise
U	648	Light beaver gray
→	703	Chartreuse
Ⓐ	704	Bright chartreuse
◎	844	Ultra dark beaver gray
©	934	Black avocado green
☰	935	Dark avocado green
S	993	Very light aquamarine
⋈	3810	Dark turquoise
U	3815	Dark celadon green
⊞	3819	Light moss green
⌐	3849	Light teal green
▼	3866	Ultra very light mocha brown

Use 6 strands of thread for backstitch.

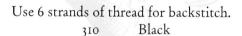

	310	Black

Red Bird

Instructions and Symbol Key

FABRIC: 14 count
STITCHES: 113 x 127
SIZE: 8.07 x 9.07 inches or 20.50 x 23.04 centimeters
COLORS: DMC

Use 2 strands of thread for cross-stitch.

SYMBOL	No.	COLOR NAME
▼	211	Light lavender
⑧	307	Lemon
◆	321	Red
⬇	519	Sky blue
◣	600	Very dark cranberry
⬇	601	Dark cranberry
↑	603	Cranberry
◢	604	Light cranberry
⊙	747	Very light sky blue
●	946	Medium burnt orange
▷	970	Light pumpkin
→	995	Dark electric blue
⋈	996	Medium electric blue
★	3072	Very light beaver gray
❼	3756	Ultra very light baby blue
#	3819	Light moss green
✪	3853	Dark autumn gold

Use 6 strands of thread for backstitch.

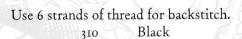

	310	Black

Dragon Head

Instructions and Symbol Key

Fabric: 14 count
Stitches: 92 x 73
Size: 6.57 x 5.21 inches or 16.69 x 13.24 centimeters
Colors: DMC

Use 2 strands of thread for cross-stitch.

Symbol	No.	Color Name
■	310	Black
E	320	Medium pistachio green
D	350	Medium coral
1	368	Light pistachio green
◿	451	Dark shell gray
Γ	452	Medium shell gray
▽	535	Very light ash gray
Ⓨ	645	Very dark beaver gray
Ⓛ	646	Dark beaver gray
E	712	Cream
N	721	Medium orange spice
Ⓐ	726	Light topaz
◧	727	Very light topaz
◆	762	Very light pearl gray
∅	844	Ultra dark beaver gray
⑦	934	Black avocado green
★	946	Medium burnt orange
C	966	Medium baby green
J	3024	Very light brown gray
⑨	3371	Ebony
Ⓙ	3857	Dark rosewood
W	3865	Winter white

Use 6 strands of thread for backstitch.
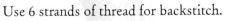

      310   Black

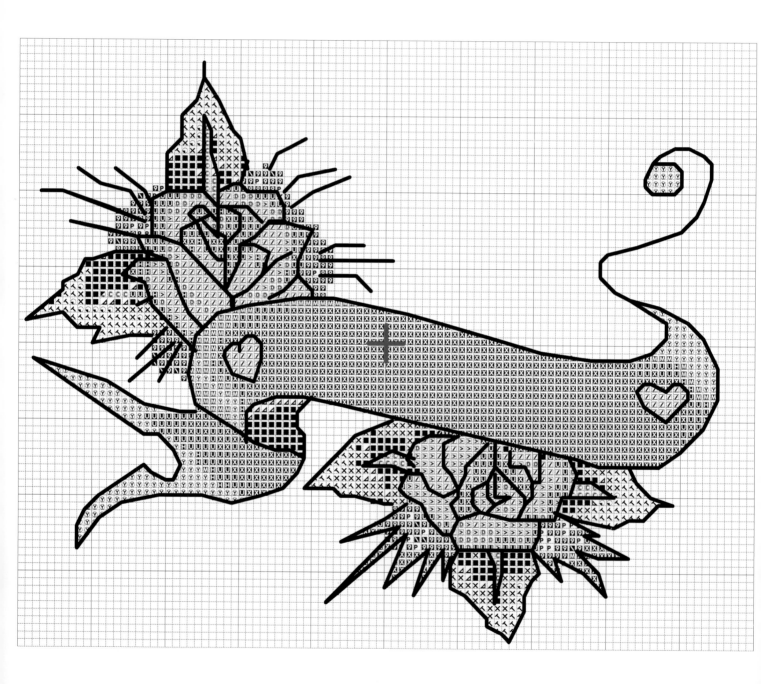

Rose Banner

Instructions and Symbol Key

Fabric: 14 count
Stitches: 94 x 76
Size: 6.71 x 5.43 inches or 17.05 x 13.79 centimeters
Colors: DMC

Use 2 strands of thread for cross-stitch.

Symbol	No.	Color Name
■	310	Black
>	352	Light coral
P	519	Sky blue
×	535	Very light ash gray
◗	646	Dark beaver gray
U	712	Cream
©	727	Very light topaz
N	747	Very light sky blue
M	762	Very light pearl gray
⊼	913	Medium Nile green
◢	934	Black avocado green
⧄	946	Medium burnt orange
Y	3743	Very light antique violet
9	3761	Light sky blue
D	3824	Light apricot
X	3865	Winter white
H	3866	Ultra very light mocha brown

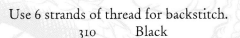

Use 6 strands of thread for backstitch.

	310	Black

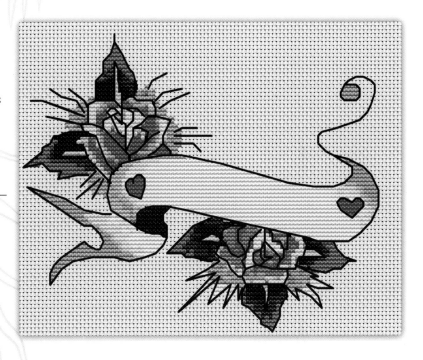

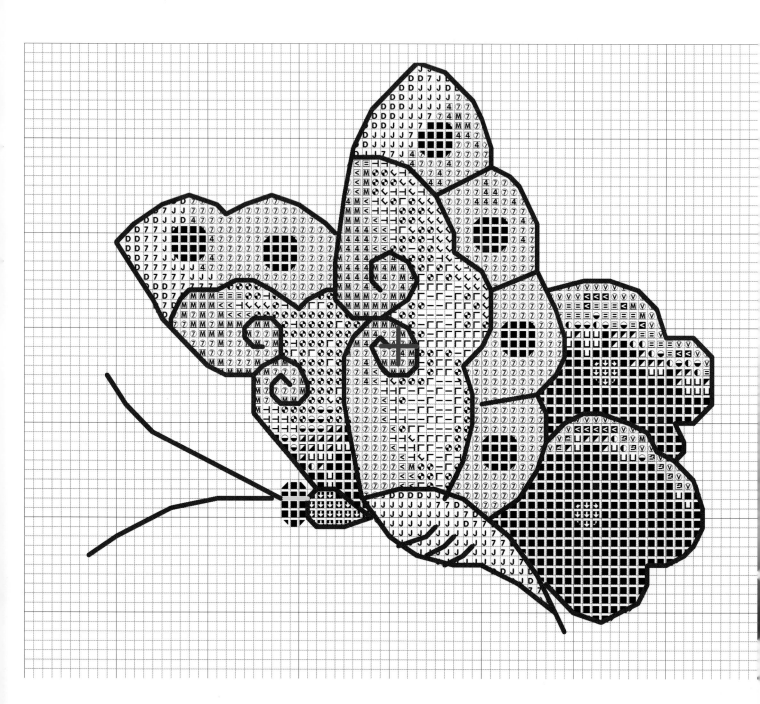

Black Butterfly

Instructions and Symbol Key

Fabric: 14 count
Stitches: 68 x 60
Size: 4.86 x 4.29 inches or 12.34 x 10.89 centimeters
Colors: DMC

Use 2 strands of thread for cross-stitch.

Symbol	No.	Color Name
⑦	307	Lemon
■	310	Black
◑	581	Moss green
D	606	Bright orange-red
◐	640	Very dark beige gray
◧	644	Medium beige gray
—	702	Kelly green
↖	704	Bright chartreuse
7	720	Dark orange spice
④	726	Light topaz
◨	730	Very dark olive green
◁	743	Medium yellow
M	744	Pale yellow
⬇	817	Very dark coral red
Γ	905	Dark parrot green
⊙	906	Medium parrot green
⊣	907	Light parrot green
⊔	934	Black avocado green
J	946	Medium burnt orange
▣	3013	Light khaki green
◪	3051	Dark green gray
Ⓥ	3823	Ultra pale yellow

Use 6 strands of thread for backstitch.

	307	Lemon
	310	Black

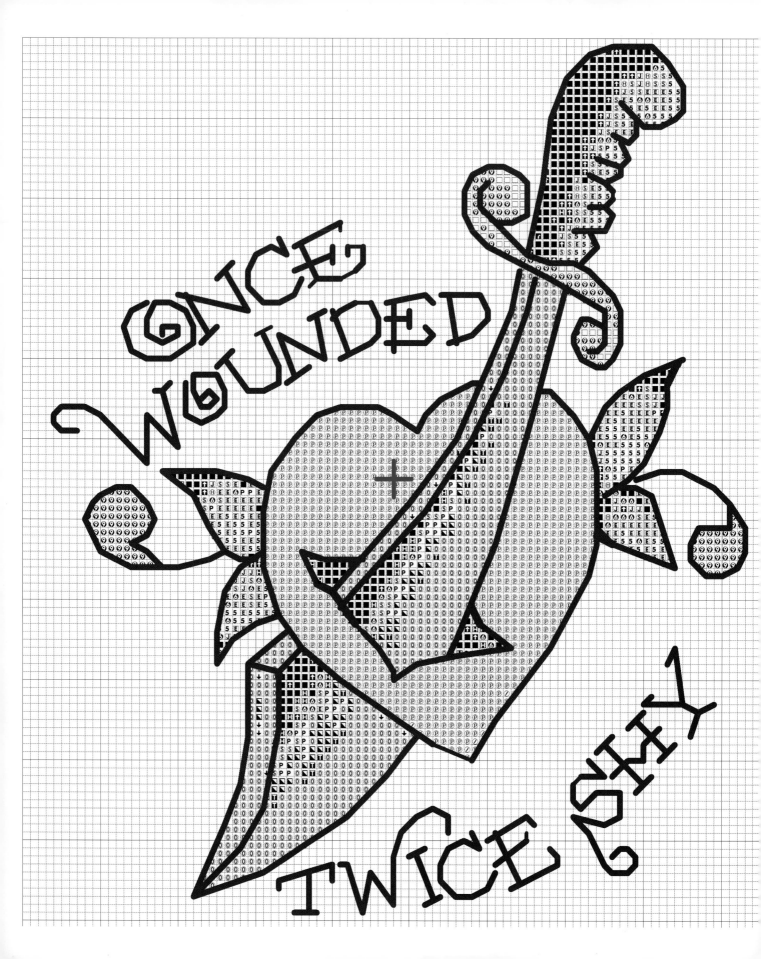

Once Wounded, Twice Shy

Instructions and Symbol Key

Fabric: 14 count
Stitches: 89 x 108
Size: 6.36 x 7.71 inches or 16.15 x 19.59 centimeters
Colors: DMC

Use 2 strands of thread for cross-stitch.

Symbol	No.	Color Name
9	307	Lemon
■	310	Black
P	372	Light mustard
5	704	Bright chartreuse
↓	712	Cream
□	725	Medium light topaz
6	730	Very dark olive green
0	822	Light beige gray
H	898	Very dark coffee brown
↑	934	Black avocado green
J	936	Very dark avocado green
P	946	Medium burnt orange
E	989	Forest green
S	3011	Dark khaki green
◣	3047	Light yellow beige
H	3362	Dark pine green
T	3866	Ultra very light mocha brown

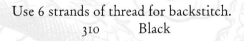

Use 6 strands of thread for backstitch.

	310	Black

Blooming Skull

Instructions and Symbol Key

FABRIC: 14 count
STITCHES: 88 x 95
SIZE: 6.29 x 6.79 inches or 15.97 x 17.24 centimeters
COLORS: DMC

Use 2 strands of thread for cross-stitch.

SYMBOL	No.	COLOR NAME
②	166	Medium light moss green
❷	307	Lemon
■	310	Black
H	352	Light coral
◐	603	Cranberry
W	604	Light cranberry
+	606	Bright orange-red
N	703	Chartreuse
J	747	Very light sky blue
E	818	Baby pink
◐	890	Ultra dark pistachio green
J	891	Dark carnation
←	905	Dark parrot green
V	956	Geranium
4	964	Light seagreen
↓	3688	Medium mauve
◑	3689	Light mauve
❶	3756	Ultra very light baby blue
D	3806	Light cyclamen pink
T	White	White

Use 6 strands of thread for backstitch.

	310	Black

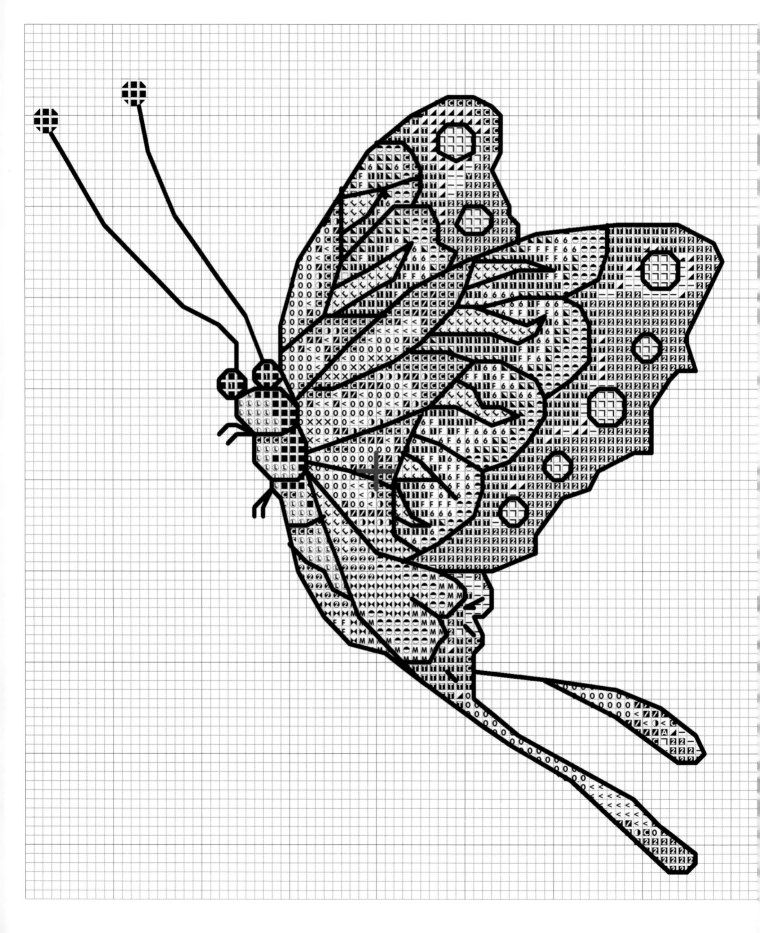

Rainbow Butterfly

Instructions and Symbol Key

FABRIC: 14 count
STITCHES: 78 x 87
SIZE: 5.57 x 6.21 inches or 14.15 x 15.78 centimeters
COLORS: DMC

Use 2 strands of thread for cross-stitch.

SYMBOL	No.	COLOR NAME
❷	210	Medium lavender
⋈	211	Light lavender
■	310	Black
⌄	327	Dark violet
✕	336	Navy blue
⊤	702	Kelly green
◢	703	Chartreuse
●	712	Cream
◖	762	Very light pearl gray
○	798	Dark delft blue
＜	809	Delft blue
─	907	Light parrot green
▮	961	Dark dusty rose
F	962	Medium dusty rose
⌐	3348	Light yellow green
6	3354	Light dusty rose
◣	3689	Light mauve
◑	3753	Ultra very light antique blue
❷	3819	Light moss green
⧄	3840	Light lavender blue
ⓛ	3860	Cocoa
M	White	White

Use 6 strands of thread for backstitch.

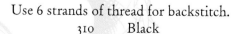

310	Black

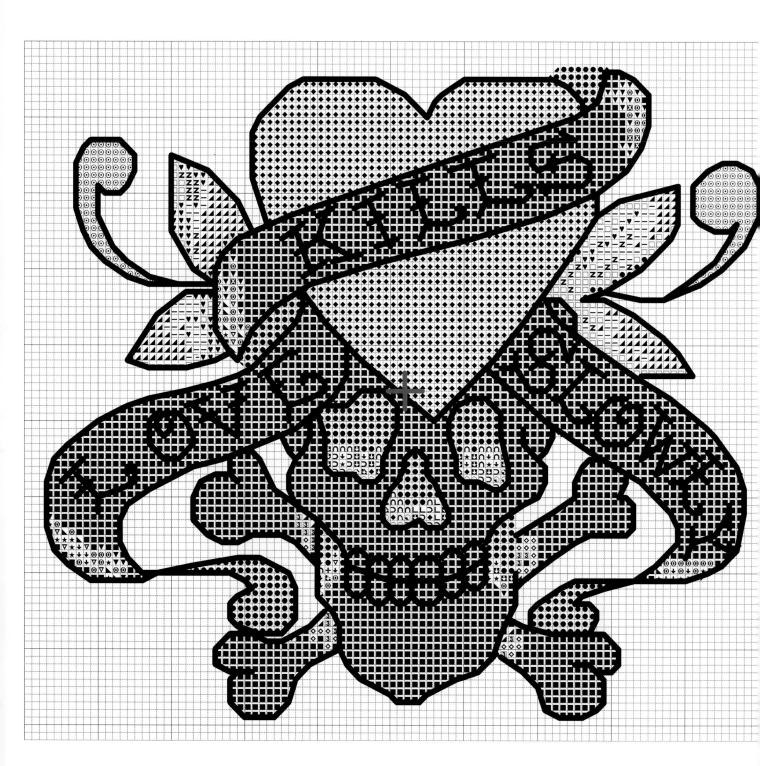

Love Kills Slowly

Instructions and Symbol Key

Fabric: 14 count
Stitches: 97 x 86
Size: 6.93 x 6.14 inches or 17.60 x 15.60 centimeters
Colors: DMC

Use 2 strands of thread for cross-stitch.

Symbol	No.	Color Name
●	310	Black
♥	319	Very dark pistachio green
◇	369	Very light pistachio green
L	434	Light brown
↓	640	Very dark beige gray
⊙	728	Topaz
⓪	739	Ultra very light tan
■	746	Off white
⊠	822	Light beige gray
▽	842	Very light beige brown
□	890	Ultra dark pistachio green
◆	900	Dark burnt orange
⊃	920	Medium copper
◖	922	Light copper
Z	986	Very dark forest green
―	987	Dark forest green
◢	988	Medium forest green
③	989	Forest green
◣	3033	Very light mocha brown
⬒	3778	Light terra cotta
★	3782	Light mocha brown
∩	3787	Dark brown gray
▼	Ecru	Ecru

Use 6 strands of thread for backstitch.
310   Black

Lil' Devil

Instructions and Symbol Key

Fabric: 14 count
Stitches: 75 x 100
Size: 5.36 x 7.14 inches or 13.61 x 18.14 centimeters
Colors: DMC

Use 2 strands of thread for cross-stitch.

Symbol	No.	Color Name
⬆	154	Very dark grape
●	310	Black
7	350	Medium coral
M	400	Dark mahogany
J	453	Light shell gray
⬆	535	Very light ash gray
⊤	646	Dark beaver gray
↓	647	Medium beaver gray
➤	648	Light beaver gray
0	712	Cream
H	720	Dark orange spice
T	844	Ultra dark beaver gray
0	898	Very dark coffee brown
P	900	Dark burnt orange
3	919	Red copper
⋈	920	Medium copper
V	921	Copper
/	922	Light copper
◄	3822	Light straw
⑦	3857	Dark rosewood
4	3866	Ultra very light mocha brown

Use 6 strands of thread for backstitch.

| | 310 | Black |

25

Death of Love

Instructions and Symbol Key

Fabric: 14 count
Stitches: 76 x 110
Size: 5.43 x 7.86 inches or 13.79 x 19.96 centimeters
Colors: DMC

Use 2 strands of thread for cross-stitch.

Symbol	No.	Color Name
–	165	Very light moss green
⊘	310	Black
7	349	Dark coral
>	535	Very light ash gray
P	606	Bright orange-red
N	644	Medium beige gray
2	677	Very light old gold
V	712	Cream
>	720	Dark orange spice
W	733	Medium olive green
✓	734	Light olive green
C	900	Dark burnt orange
L	3033	Very light mocha brown
⊙	3810	Dark turquoise
M	3813	Light blue green

Use 6 strands of thread for backstitch.

	310	Black

L. A. Panther

Instructions and Symbol Key

Fabric: 14 count
Stitches: 91 x 67
Size: 6.50 x 4.79 inches or 16.51 x 12.16 centimeters
Colors: DMC

Use 2 strands of thread for cross-stitch.

Symbol	No.	Color Name
7	307	Lemon
■	310	Black
T	415	Pearl gray
Z	451	Dark shell gray
♥	535	Very light ash gray
J	603	Cranberry
V	605	Very light cranberry
⌐	646	Dark beaver gray
≡	647	Medium beaver gray
4	648	Light beaver gray
⅃	712	Cream
2	720	Dark orange spice
◄	762	Very light pearl gray
✕	898	Very dark coffee brown
1	900	Dark burnt orange
0	928	Very light gray green
L	934	Black avocado green
●	939	Very dark navy blue
E	947	Burnt orange
⋈	3021	Very dark brown gray
M	3023	Light brown gray
Y	3024	Very light brown gray
▷	3072	Very light beaver gray
⊙	3341	Apricot
U	3787	Dark brown gray
6	White	White

Use 6 strands of thread for backstitch.

	310	Black

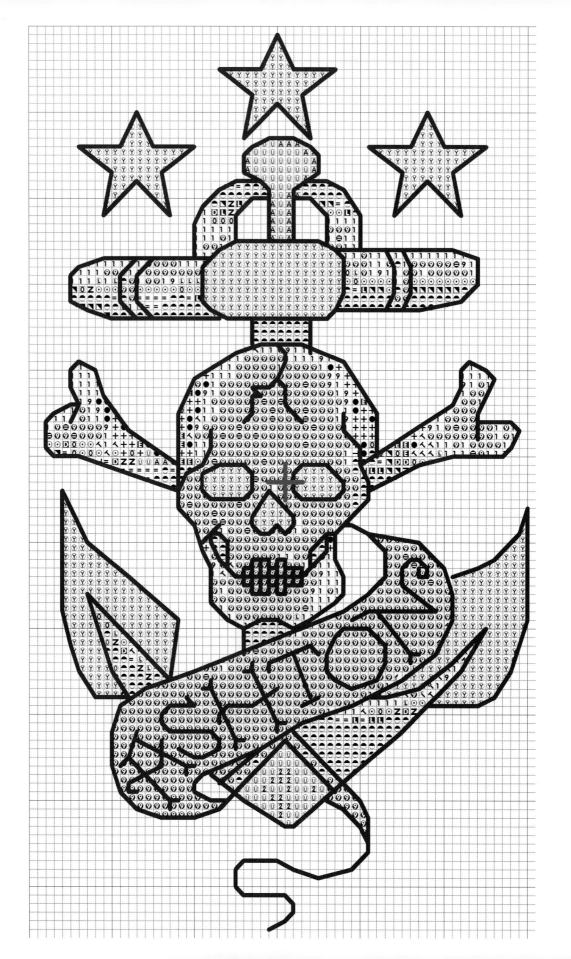

Skull 'n' Anchor

Instructions and Symbol Key

Fabric: 14 count
Stitches: 58 x 104
Size: 4.14 x 7.43 inches or 10.52 x 18.87 centimeters
Colors: DMC

Use 2 strands of thread for cross-stitch.

Symbol	No.	Color Name
◎	154	Very dark grape
◒	310	Black
E	368	Light pistachio green
●	369	Very light pistachio green
A	562	Medium jade
=	646	Dark beaver gray
Z	647	Medium beaver gray
Z	648	Light beaver gray
1	712	Cream
2	912	Light emerald green
U	913	Medium Nile green
Y	946	Medium burnt orange
+	966	Medium baby green
N	3022	Medium brown gray
D	3023	Light brown gray
⊙	3024	Very light brown gray
⊼	3072	Very light beaver gray
L	3787	Dark brown gray
θ	3865	Winter white
L	3866	Ultra very light mocha brown
9	Ecru	Ecru
⊖	White	White

Use 6 strands of thread for backstitch.

	310	Black

Spider Skull

Instructions and Symbol Key

FABRIC: 14 count
STITCHES: 93 x 106
SIZE: 6.64 x 7.57 inches or 16.87 x 19.23 centimeters
COLORS: DMC

Use 2 strands of thread for cross-stitch.

SYMBOL	NO.	COLOR NAME
⊗	165	Very light moss green
■	310	Black
7	371	Mustard
>	372	Light mustard
⬆	469	Avocado green
⫽	470	Light avocado green
⊘	472	Ultra light avocado green
⌐	520	Dark fern green
0	581	Moss green
9	606	Bright orange-red
⩘	611	Drab brown
c	612	Light drab brown
6	642	Dark beige gray
V	704	Bright chartreuse
⬚	730	Very dark olive green
◢	822	Light beige gray
★	906	Medium parrot green
s	907	Light parrot green
⊔	934	Black avocado green
∩	935	Dark avocado green
#	936	Very dark avocado green
←	3011	Dark khaki green
⟍	3012	Medium khaki green
V	3013	Light khaki green
Ⓐ	3046	Medium yellow beige
C	3345	Dark hunter green
+	3371	Black brown
◣	3787	Dark brown gray
⬆	3819	Light moss green

Use 6 strands of thread for backstitch.
　　　　310　　　　Black

Flaming Skull

Instructions and Symbol Key

Fabric: 14 count
Stitches: 61 x 101
Size: 4.36 x 7.21 inches or 11.07 x 18.32 centimeters
Colors: DMC

Use 2 strands of thread for cross-stitch.

Symbol	No.	Color Name
◪	307	Lemon
Ⓓ	310	Black
Ⓛ	413	Dark pewter gray
Ⓤ	606	Bright orange-red
<	608	Bright orange
④	700	Bright green
Ⓩ	726	Light topaz
❼	740	Tangerine
Ⓦ	741	Medium tangerine
·	762	Very light pearl gray
Ⓐ	911	Medium emerald green
9	926	Medium gray green
④	927	Light gray green
❾	928	Very light gray green
Ⓗ	946	Medium burnt orange
Ⓛ	947	Burnt orange
Ⓩ	954	Nile green
=	967	Very light apricot
Ⓤ	3340	Medium apricot
Ⓖ	3341	Apricot
◮	3756	Ultra very light baby blue
Ⓢ	3799	Very dark pewter gray
⅂	White	White

Use 6 strands of thread for backstitch.
| | 310 | Black |

Gambling Man

Instructions and Symbol Key

FABRIC: 14 count
STITCHES: 84 x 101
SIZE: 6.00 x 7.21 inches or 15.24 x 18.32 centimeters
COLORS: DMC

Use 2 strands of thread for cross-stitch.

SYMBOL	No.	COLOR NAME
1	166	Medium light moss green
■	310	Black
▽	563	Light jade
S	606	Bright orange-red
⋈	746	Off white
7	747	Very light sky blue
⌐	833	Light golden olive
T	890	Ultra dark pistachio green
↖	905	Dark parrot green
Z	907	Light parrot green
4	955	Light Nile green
◣	964	Light seagreen
◤	973	Bright canary
Ⓜ	3756	Ultra very light baby blue
S	3818	Ultra very dark emerald green
4	3819	Light moss green
N	3823	Ultra pale yellow
V	3846	Light bright turquoise
⊖	White	White

Use 6 strands of thread for backstitch.

	310	Black

Black Rose and Dagger

Instructions and Symbol Key

Fabric: 14 count
Stitches: 77 x 113
Size: 5.50 x 8.07 inches or 13.97 x 20.50 centimeters
Colors: DMC

Use 2 strands of thread for cross-stitch.

Symbol	No.	Color Name
■	310	Black
◊	452	Medium shell gray
—	505	Jade green
4	524	Very light fern green
E	606	Bright orange-red
←	640	Very dark beige gray
⦀	642	Dark beige gray
7	644	Medium beige gray
◑	645	Very dark beaver gray
U	699	Green
⌐	701	Light green
2	746	Off white
L	822	Light beige gray
↑	900	Dark burnt orange
T	910	Dark emerald green
L	912	Light emerald green
>	922	Light copper
L	934	Black avocado green
⊕	973	Bright canary
⊕	3013	Light khaki green
⬇	3021	Very dark brown gray
©	3023	Light brown gray
6	3024	Very light brown gray
⅃	3033	Very light mocha brown
✕	3362	Dark pine green
⋈	3818	Ultra very dark emerald green
S	3866	Ultra very light mocha brown
T	Ecru	Ecru

Use 6 strands of thread for backstitch.

	310	Black

The 13th Skull

Instructions and Symbol Key

FABRIC: 14 count
STITCHES: 79 x 97
SIZE: 5.64 x 6.93 inches or 14.33 x 17.60 centimeters
COLORS: DMC

Use 2 strands of thread for cross-stitch.

SYMBOL	No.	COLOR NAME
◖	310	Black
Ⓛ	333	Very dark blue violet
5	472	Ultra light avocado green
7	535	Very light ash gray
☐	640	Very dark beige gray
◪	644	Medium beige gray
Ⓥ	721	Medium orange spice
6	739	Ultra very light tan
≡	746	Off white
Ⓛ	842	Very light beige brown
P	900	Dark burnt orange
N	3021	Very dark brown gray
Ⱶ	3022	Medium brown gray
▼	3023	Light brown gray
▽	3047	Light yellow beige
E	3787	Dark brown gray
⊕	3819	Light moss green
◒	3823	Ultra pale yellow
◇	3855	Light autumn gold
◣	3865	Winter white
∩	Ecru	Ecru
4	White	White

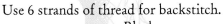

Use 6 strands of thread for backstitch.

	310	Black

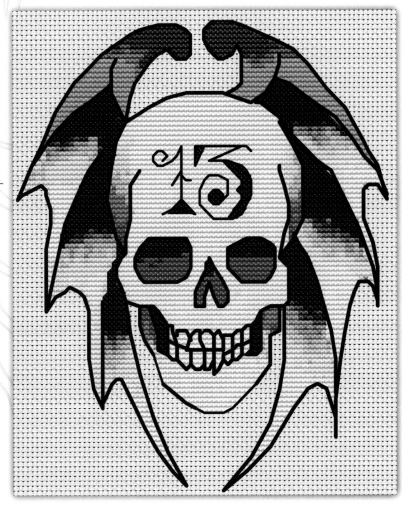

Royal Tiger

Instructions and Symbol Key

Fabric: 14 count
Stitches: 110 x 119
Size: 7.86 x 8.50 inches or 19.96 x 21.59 centimeters
Colors: DMC

Use 2 strands of thread for cross-stitch.

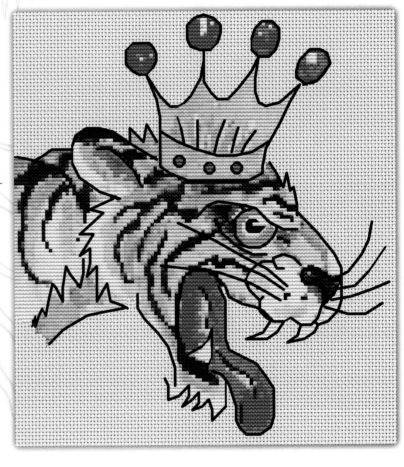

Symbol	No.	Color Name
C	209	Dark lavender
■	310	Black
0	352	Light coral
▽	535	Very light ash gray
⊜	606	Bright orange-red
3	611	Drab brown
W	648	Light beaver gray
<	712	Cream
D	721	Medium orange spice
←	726	Light topaz
P	727	Very light topaz
6	728	Topaz
4	743	Medium yellow
←	745	Light pale yellow
5	746	Off white
/	762	Very light pearl gray
◁	830	Dark golden olive
X	844	Ultra dark beaver gray
S	869	Very dark hazelnut brown
▶	898	Very dark coffee brown
2	934	Black avocado green
◖	938	Ultra dark coffee brown
F	951	Light tawny
M	3021	Very dark brown gray
★	3046	Medium yellow beige
P	3078	Very light golden yellow
V	3340	Medium apricot
Γ	3371	Black brown
↗	3781	Dark mocha brown
0	3811	Very light turquoise
X	3823	Ultra pale yellow
↓	3828	Hazelnut brown
J	3854	Medium autumn gold
◢	3855	Light autumn gold
Ⓐ	3863	Medium mocha beige
U	Ecru	Ecru
◖	White	White

Use 6 strands of thread for backstitch.

310   Black

Skull and Roses

Instructions and Symbol Key

Fabric: 14 count
Stitches: 97 x 98
Size: 6.93 x 7.00 inches or 17.60 x 17.78 centimeters
Colors: DMC

Use 2 strands of thread for cross-stitch.

Symbol	No.	Color Name
S	169	Light pewter
0	307	Lemon
■	310	Black
D	321	Red
☉	352	Light coral
←	535	Very light ash gray
7	598	Light turquoise
5	606	Bright orange-red
0	666	Bright red
L	712	Cream
7	747	Very light sky blue
8	818	Baby pink
L	819	Light baby pink
◩	890	Ultra dark pistachio green
1	907	Light parrot green
\	934	Black avocado green
☑	946	Medium burnt orange
J	3072	Very light beaver gray
M	3326	Light rose
=	3345	Dark hunter green
2	3705	Dark melon
◪	3753	Ultra very light antique blue
W	3756	Ultra very light baby blue
Z	3819	Light moss green
◨	White	White

Use 6 strands of thread for backstitch.

	310	Black

Red Rose

Instructions and Symbol Key

FABRIC: 14 count
STITCHES: 105 x 103
SIZE: 7.50 x 7.36 inches or 19.05 x 18.69 centimeters
COLORS: DMC

Use 2 strands of thread for cross-stitch.

SYMBOL	No.	COLOR NAME
❾	224	Very light shell pink
■	310	Black
5	349	Dark coral
⑨	356	Medium terra cotta
↑	520	Dark fern green
\	543	Ultra very light beige brown
F	702	Kelly green
⚼	703	Chartreuse
②	712	Cream
—	739	Ultra very light tan
Ⓨ	760	Salmon
◄	900	Dark burnt orange
→	905	Dark parrot green
⫽	934	Black avocado green
=	986	Very dark forest green
⊔	3033	Very light mocha brown
◨	3712	Medium salmon
3	3733	Dusty rose
↑	3832	Medium raspberry

Use 6 strands of thread for backstitch.

    310   Black

Black Cross

Instructions and Symbol Key

FABRIC: 14 count
STITCHES: 84 x 101
SIZE: 6.00 x 7.21 inches or 15.24 x 18.32 centimeters
COLORS: DMC

Use 2 strands of thread for cross-stitch.

SYMBOL	No.	COLOR NAME
■	310	Black
❶	318	Light steel gray
H	505	Jade green
◁	535	Very light ash gray
◿	646	Dark beaver gray
◢	647	Medium beaver gray
◣	648	Light beaver gray
Z	712	Cream
N	720	Dark orange spice
▷	721	Medium orange spice
9	726	Light topaz
N	762	Very light pearl gray
℗	928	Very light gray green
U	946	Medium burnt orange
▫	3024	Very light brown gray
P	3072	Very light beaver gray
Ⓝ	3743	Very light antique violet
◪	3761	Light sky blue
T	3844	Dark bright turquoise
S	3865	Winter white
8	3866	Ultra very light mocha brown

Use 6 strands of thread for backstitch.
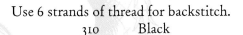

	310	Black

Love Dies Hard

Instructions and Symbol Key

Fabric: 14 count
Stitches: 95 x 139
Size: 6.79 x 9.93 inches or 17.24 x 25.22 centimeters
Colors: DMC

Use 2 strands of thread for cross-stitch.

Symbol	No.	Color Name
9	164	Light forest green
⌐	210	Medium lavender
L	307	Lemon
■	310	Black
⬇	318	Light steel gray
◁▷	606	Bright orange-red
1	712	Cream
+	726	Light topaz
1	762	Very light pearl gray
3	815	Medium garnet
②	928	Very light gray green
⬇	954	Nile green
N	955	Light Nile green
J	973	Bright canary
⌐	988	Medium forest green
←	3022	Medium brown gray
W	3072	Very light beaver gray
\	3078	Very light golden yellow
⊢	3705	Dark melon
U	3756	Ultra very light baby blue
⑤	3865	Winter white

Use 6 strands of thread for backstitch.

| | 310 | Black |

51

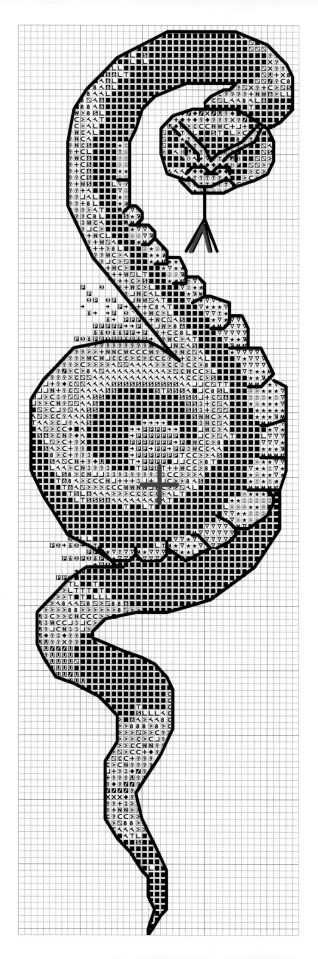

Black Snake

Instructions and Symbol Key

Fabric: 14 count
Stitches: 42 x 140
Size: 3.00 x 10.00 inches or 7.62 x 25.40 centimeters
Colors: DMC

Use 2 strands of thread for cross-stitch.

Symbol	No.	Color Name
■	310	Black
P	349	Dark coral
⁊	369	Very light pistachio green
⌐	523	Light fern green
③	524	Very light fern green
6	606	Bright orange-red
≥	640	Very dark beige gray
C	642	Dark beige gray
⑨	644	Medium beige gray
⊠	645	Very dark beaver gray
⊜	702	Kelly green
Ⓣ	703	Chartreuse
Ⓗ	727	Very light topaz
◆	772	Very light yellow green
→	817	Very dark coral red
U	822	Light beige gray
Ⓢ	900	Dark burnt orange
★	905	Dark parrot green
▽	906	Medium parrot green
L	934	Black avocado green
S	935	Dark avocado green
6	936	Very dark avocado green
8	3011	Dark khaki green
+	3013	Light khaki green
W	3032	Medium mocha brown
X	3047	Light yellow beige
⌃	3051	Dark green gray
C	3052	Medium green gray
N	3053	Green gray
T	3371	Black brown
M	3865	Winter white

Use 6 strands of thread for backstitch.

	310	Black
	349	Dark coral

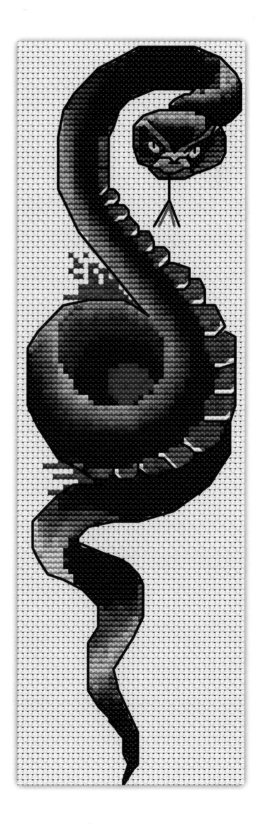

Rose-Wrapped Heart

Instructions and Symbol Key

Fabric: 14 count
Stitches: 63 x 133
Size: 4.50 x 9.50 inches or 11.43 x 24.13 centimeters
Colors: DMC

Use 2 strands of thread for cross-stitch.

Symbol	No.	Color Name
④	307	Lemon
■	310	Black
⑧	608	Bright orange
1	700	Bright green
O	702	Kelly green
U	721	Medium orange spice
⑨	722	Light orange spice
Ↄ	746	Off white
✕	895	Very dark hunter green
5	911	Medium emerald green
Ⓨ	912	Light emerald green
Ⓟ	938	Ultra dark coffee brown
Ⓞ	946	Medium burnt orange
8	951	Light tawny
⤧	3340	Medium apricot
⬐	3787	Dark brown gray
N	3818	Ultra very dark emerald green
⑧	3823	Ultra pale yellow
▣	3825	Pale pumpkin
☐	3865	Winter white

Use 6 strands of thread for backstitch.

	310	Black

Bulldog King

Instructions and Symbol Key

FABRIC: 14 count
STITCHES: 70 x 85
SIZE: 5.00 x 6.07 inches or 12.70 x 15.42 centimeters
COLORS: DMC

Use 2 strands of thread for cross-stitch.

SYMBOL	No.	COLOR NAME
ⒽΞ	307	Lemon
■	310	Black
—	400	Dark mahogany
Ⓜ	445	Light lemon
▤	606	Bright orange-red
◇	702	Kelly green
♥	741	Medium tangerine
◣	780	Ultra very dark topaz
⋈	814	Dark garnet
8	906	Medium parrot green
◗	927	Light gray green
◆	938	Ultra dark coffee brown
#	951	Light tawny
●	3031	Very dark mocha brown
✕	3345	Dark hunter green
▼	3853	Dark autumn gold
⊙	3856	Ultra very light mahogany
⋈	3865	Winter white
◩	5200	Snow white

Use 6 strands of thread for backstitch.

	310	Black

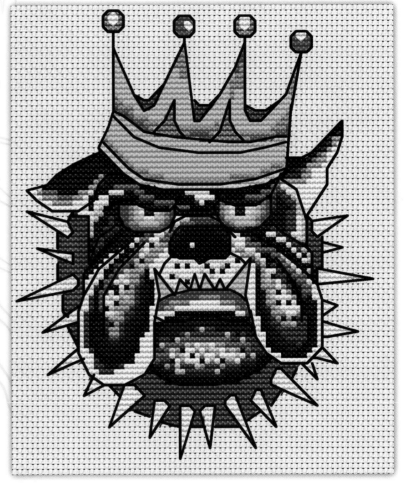

Flower and Diamond Banner

Instructions and Symbol Key

Fabric: 14 count
Stitches: 99 x 142
Size: 7.07 x 10.14 inches or 17.96 x 25.76 centimeters
Colors: DMC

Use 2 strands of thread for cross-stitch.

Symbol	No.	Color Name
■	310	Black
4	347	Very dark salmon
H	350	Medium coral
8	351	Coral
③	352	Light coral
D	606	Bright orange-red
V	743	Medium yellow
3	747	Very light sky blue
1	754	Light peach
⑦	758	Very light terra cotta
N	761	Light salmon
T	818	Baby pink
6	900	Dark burnt orange
○	909	Very dark emerald green
◑	911	Medium emerald green
▼	934	Black avocado green
▬	966	Medium baby green
◢	991	Dark aquamarine
>	3761	Light sky blue
▶◀	3850	Dark bright green
➜	3851	Light bright green
⌐	3859	Light rosewood
❺	White	White

Use 6 strands of thread for backstitch.

	310	Black
	818	Baby pink

Tiger Head

Instructions and Symbol Key

Fabric: 14 count
Stitches: 104 x 96
Size: 7.43 x 6.86 inches or 18.87 x 17.42 centimeters
Colors: DMC

Use 2 strands of thread for cross-stitch.

Symbol	No.	Color Name
1	307	Lemon
■	310	Black
◐	400	Dark mahogany
◢	444	Dark lemon
⊘	603	Cranberry
P	606	Bright orange-red
★	647	Medium beaver gray
←	677	Very light old gold
J	712	Cream
0	721	Medium orange spice
×	726	Light topaz
1	741	Medium tangerine
☯	780	Ultra very dark topaz
⊠	783	Medium topaz
↘	832	Golden olive
8	898	Very dark coffee brown
V	913	Medium Nile green
N	934	Black avocado green
8	936	Very dark avocado green
⊠	946	Medium burnt orange
⋈	947	Burnt orange
0	973	Bright canary
5	3072	Very light beaver gray
\	3371	Black brown
℗	3853	Dark autumn gold
Y	3865	Winter white

Use 6 strands of thread for backstitch.

	310	Black

A A A M B B

C C D D D

E E F F G

G H H H H I I

Ed Hardy Alphabet

Instructions and Symbol Key

Fabric: 14 count
Stitches: 607 x 192
Size: 43.36 x 13.71 inches or 110.13 x 34.83 centimeters
Colors: DMC

No.	Color Name
Use 6 strands of thread for backstitch.	
310	Black

A A A B B B C C
D D D E E F F
G G H H H I I
J J K K K L L
M M M M
N N N N N O O O
P P Q Q R R
S S S T T
U U U U U V V
W W W X X X
Y Y Y Z Z Z Z

J J J K K

K L L L M

M M M M

N N N N N

O O O P P

Q Q R R

S S S T T

U U U U U

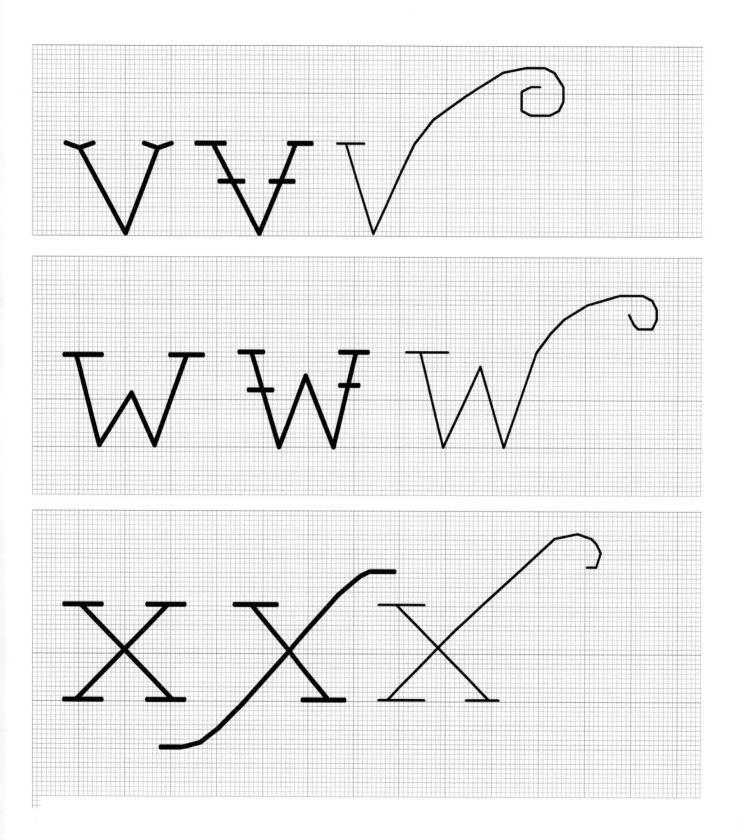

Y Y Y Z

Z Z Z

Original Images

Three Hearts Dagger

Blue Bird

Blue
Butterfly

Red Bird

Dragon Head

Rose Banner

Black Butterfly

ONCE WOUNDED

TWICE SHY

Once Wounded,
Twice Shy

Blooming Skull

Rainbow Butterfly

Love
Kills Slowly

Lil'Devil

IRA

Death of Love

L. A. Panther

Skull 'n' Anchor

Spider Skull

Flaming Skull

13

FREE FOREVER

Gambling Man

A

Black Rose
and Dagger

THE CORPS

The 13th Skull

Royal Tiger

Skull and Roses

Red Rose

Black Cross

Love Dies Hard

Black Snake

Rose-Wrapped Heart

Bulldog King

Flower and
Diamond Banner

Tiger Head